Introduction

In today's dynamic and ever-evolving business landscape, the ability to effectively manage a portfolio of corporate initiatives has become not just a strategic imperative but a defining characteristic of successful organizations. The world of business is no longer a simple, linear path; it is a complex web of projects, products, and services, all intertwined in a delicate dance of innovation, resource allocation, and risk management. The Portfolio Management and Product Strategy is one part that leads into the 5P success for company growth and development.

1 Portfolio strategy and products

- Redefine product portfolio—eg, withdraw some products, introduce new products
- Revise pricing in line with purpose
- Review portfolio and test purposefulness of individual assets against common criteria

2 People and culture

- Align recruiting, people development, and career pathways to enable purpose
- Define purpose KPIs and hold employees accountable/give them incentives to meet targets
- Articulate and role-model desired individual mindsets and behaviors linked to purpose

3 Processes and systems

- Adapt operational processes to meet purpose-related targets
- Ensure supplier behaviors are in line with purpose

4 Performance metrics

- Set performance targets and metrics in line with purpose
- Introduce capital-allocation metrics in line with purpose for decisions (eg, capital expenditures, M&A)

5 Positions and engagements

- Tailor external engagement and communications to purpose
- Revise external positions in line with purpose
- Align affiliations (eg, trade-association membership) with purpose

PURPOSE

McKinsey & Company

Figure 1: McKinsey the 5P model[1]

As we embark on this journey through the world of corporate portfolio management, we find ourselves at a crucial juncture in the history of business. The rapid pace of technological advancement, the shifting sands of global markets, and the increasing demands of stakeholders

---

[1] McKinsey (2022), More than a mission statement: How the 5Ps embed purpose to deliver value, McKinsey Quaterly

have all converged to create an environment where traditional approaches to management are no longer sufficient.

This book is an exploration of the art and science of corporate portfolio management. It delves into the strategies, techniques, and best practices that can help organizations navigate the intricate terrain of their project and initiative portfolios. From aligning portfolios with strategic goals to optimizing resource allocation, from assessing and mitigating risks to fostering innovation, this book provides a comprehensive guide to mastering the complexities of modern corporate portfolio management.

In the following chapters, we will explore the fundamental principles of corporate portfolio management, dissect the key components of a successful portfolio, and uncover the strategies that can help organizations thrive in an era of constant change. We will also examine the role of technology, data analytics, and organizational culture in shaping portfolio management practices.

Above all, this book is an invitation to embark on a journey of discovery, to unlock the potential of corporate portfolio management as a powerful tool for achieving strategic objectives and driving sustainable growth. The challenges are immense, but so are the opportunities. Join us as we navigate the intricate world of corporate portfolio management, and let's embark on this transformative journey together.

Contents

Introduction to Portfolio Management

In this foundational chapter, readers will gain a comprehensive understanding of the role and importance of portfolio management in the context of corporate enterprises. Key concepts such as portfolio optimization, risk management, and strategic alignment will be introduced. The chapter will also outline the structure of the book and provide an overview of what readers can expect to learn throughout the following chapters.

The Significance of Portfolio Management

Portfolio management is a critical discipline that plays a pivotal role in the success of corporate enterprises. At its core, it is the art and science of making strategic investment decisions to achieve specific organizational objectives. The concept of portfolio management draws inspiration from the world of finance, where investors diversify their investments to spread risk and optimize returns. In the context of corporate enterprise, portfolio management is about selecting, prioritizing, and managing a collection of projects, programs, and initiatives that collectively contribute to the realization of the company's strategic goals.

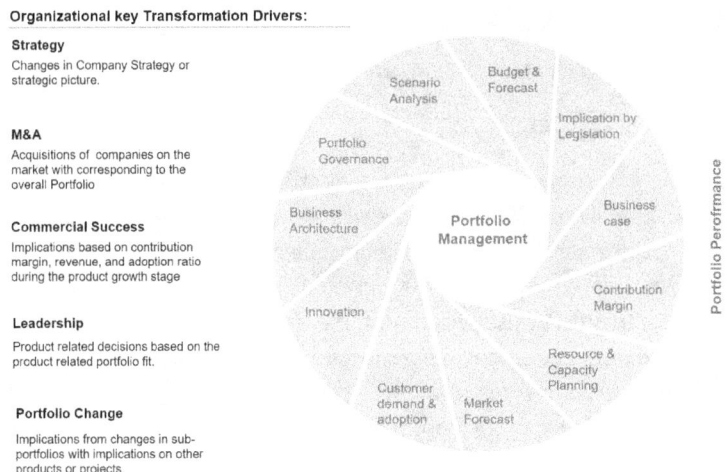

Figure 2: The integrated Portfolio cycle

Portfolio strategy assesses investment and divestment options and their implications for capital on a variety of different solutions, projects, customer branches or products. Portfolio Management could be adopted to all these different levels to identify, review and adjust the portfolio including decisions on spend and the portfolio related path forward. The Portfolio allows to research products or technologies in any stage to define the strategic long term planning for a company considering the next 2 or more years Based on the portfolio management process the company can adjust the planned development opportunities including future revenue streams, budget plans and cost allocation for their entire portfolio. The decision roadmap that – a corporate needs to follow at the end of the portfolio review cycle is to decide on Capital deployed in existing business, capital deployed in larger investment opportunities and capital that is gained by existing exiting existing businesses. In any of the scenarios outlined above Portfolio Management allows Leaders to make better and informed decisions.

The Portfolio Management Process

Understanding the portfolio management process is essential for grasping its significance. Portfolio Management applies for different kind of solutions, products, projects or industries. This process typically involves several key stages:

Identification and Definition:

In this initial stage, organizations identify potential projects and initiatives that align with their strategic objectives. These opportunities are evaluated in terms of their feasibility, alignment with the company's mission, and potential benefits. Additional influencing factors are also external factors that raise based on the external information received. This could be market related movements e.g. towards green technology for existing products or legal implications to review the existing portfolio and decide on the products that support the future growth stages. Thinking about tooling would be the SWOT or PESTLE Analysis.[2]

---

[2] SWOT: Philip Kotler, Roland Berger und Nils Rickhoff: The Quintessence of Strategic Management. Springer-Verlag: Berlin 2010, S.   30.

The SWOT analysis has an internal and external focus whereas the PESTLE Analysis is focused only on 6 legal and environmental factors. The SWOT analysis has been developed back in the 1960s by Harvard Business School.

SWOT: S - Strengthen, W - Weakness, O - Opportunities, T- Threats

The general intention of the SWOT analysis. The SWOT with its external and internal attributes allows to identify if the company's strategy allows or hinders the companies achievement of its vision. The Aim is that the company's strategy leverages internal strength to combine them with external opportunities while using strength to manage threats. This will lead to a result of future market segments, new partners required, products that need to be adjusted and investment decisions that shall be revised.[3]

The PESTLE Analysis – as outlined – is based on external factors only and allows the company mainly to drive the identification of potential achievements in the outside-in perspective.

PESTLE: P – Political, E – Economic, S- sociocultural, T – Technological, L-Legal and E for Environmental.

The Pestle analysis refers mainly to the specific fields and reflects the answers via questions e.g. "How does the political environment affect

---

PESTLE: Nandonde, Felix Adamu, A PESTLE analysis of international retailing in the East African Community, . Global Business and Organizational Excellence. Page 54–61

[3] Robert S. Kaplan and David P. Norton (2008): Matering the Management System, Harvard Business Review

the business itself?". By questioning all the different 6 layers of the Pestle analysis it will lead to areas of improvement, threats and preparation of related decisions for the company's path forward. The Economic part will lead to the understanding of all economic implications such as interest rates, inflation, exchange rate, growth rates for specific customer segments based on environmental decision, Taxes etc.

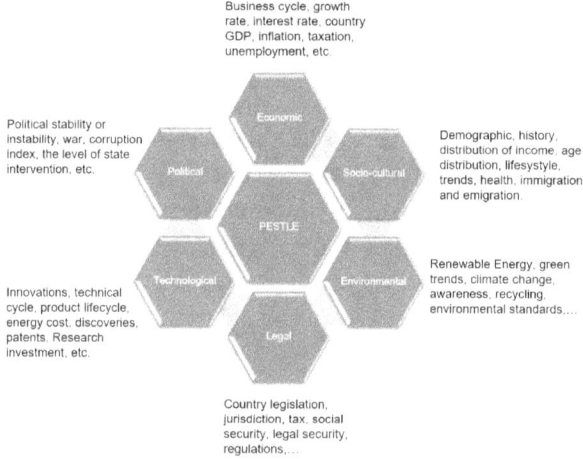

Figure 3: Approach to ellaborate on external factors with the PESTLE appraoch

The socio-cultural part is related to the consumer and the trends in society and culture. The technological aspect relates to innovations, investments in R&D, technical cycles etc.[4]

As already outlined, PESTLE only allows the external implication review on the strategic level of certain products but all these factors have direct or indirect influence to the product portfolio.

Selection and Prioritization:

Once identified, projects and initiatives are subjected to a rigorous selection and prioritization process. Factors such as return on investment, strategic alignment, resource availability, and risk are

---

[44] Del Marmol, Thomas (2016), Pestle Analysis,

considered. The goal is to determine which projects, products should be included in the portfolio and in what order they should be executed.

The major challenges in the selection and priorization cycle are the multiplied variants of objectives and input parameters that need to be followed. The are 7 fields that influence the selection process.

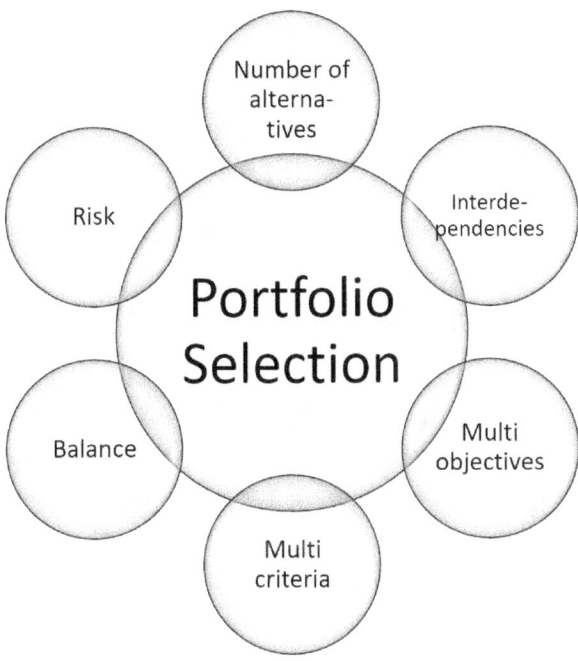

Figure 4: Portfolio Management factors

Multi-criteria: The decision criteria and the relevance of ambitions that are related to the pre-analytics executed in the SWOT or in the PESTLE analysis will interact with the multi objective corridor. Therefore, a detailed evaluation and distinction between the different types of criteria would be required. The number of alternatives is either infinite or not countable. All kind of different challenges are considered as a subclasses of Multi Criteria Decision Making problems (MCDM). The MCDM problems can also be divided into two major classes with respect to the way the weights of the alternatives are determined: Compensatory and Outranking Decision Making.[5]

Multi-objectives: The strategic planning process leads to multiple objectives with different commercial aspects and different time horizons. Objectives are also managed inside the company starting with various kind of different management tools leading to the integrated reporting based on tools that in cooperate the different angles like the Balanced Scorecard (BSC).[6]

Number of alternatives: Although the criteria and objectives may limit the number of different solution scenarios the alternatives that are elaborated on are huge based on external (e.g. political, environmental, social, et.al.) factors that influence the pre-liminary decision making and the potential combination of different alternatives towards several key objectives.

Interdependencies: Between all decision-making processes towards a portfolio structure, a simple sample is the budget that may interfere with the planned products and lead to interdependencies within the company and its product portfolio. Although the portfolio management needs to provide clear decision-making processes, the entire value chain may vary based on broad changes with investment decisions.

Risk: Every strategic decision taken by a company is having components of uncertainty that are going along with it. Therefore, the future implications of the decision need to be evaluated and – based on the related risk management approach – continuously monitored (see Chapter: Risk Management in Portfolio Management).

---

[5] Majumder, M. (2015). Multi Criteria Decision Making. In: Impact of Urbanization on Water Shortage in Face of Climatic Aberrations. Springer Briefs in Water Science and Technology. Springer, Singapore. p. 35-45

[6] Robert S. Kaplan, David P. Norton (1996), The Balanced Scorecard: Translating Strategy into Action, Harvard Business Review

Balance: In addition to maximizing the value for the company the portfolio needs to have a balance to meet future needs and ensure economic growth as one potential ambition but also balance the different angles. Another opportunity that may be seen is the Diversification of a company into different fields.

The Portfolio objectives: efficiency, balance, and strategic effectiveness.

Planning and Execution:

After selection, the projects and initiatives are planned and executed according to predefined timelines, budgets, and objectives. Effective project management practices are employed to ensure successful execution. The planning process of all portfolio activities can be done based on certain tools that continuously monitor the products or projects against the business case related objectives that delivered the baseline for the entire decision-making process. This continuous review is necessary to track the transformation and success of the product evolution and the entire product lifecycle. All these activities require continuous tracking across the entire product lifecycle to ensure that – every touchpoint and every stage that a product passes the appropriate review and action is taken.

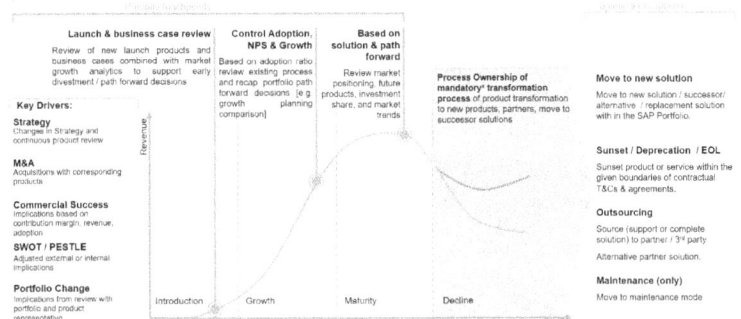

Figure 5: Product lifecycle and corporate actions

The continuous lifecycle monitoring allows to act quickly in every stage of transformation and ensure that the appropriate measures are taken (e.g. move to another solution, deprecation, divestment, etc.).

Monitoring and Control:

Portfolio managers continuously monitor the progress of solutions, products, projects and initiatives within the portfolio. They assess performance against established criteria, identify issues, and take corrective actions as needed. This stage is crucial for ensuring that the portfolio remains aligned with the organization's strategic goals. Therefore certain Key Performance Indicators (KPIs) are required to define the evaluation methodology and ensure that every product can be compared against each other to have a neutral baseline.

A simple way is to track the performance against the planned evolution of the product or the related business case and adjust it based on the individual success compared to the original objectives. That is similar to the monitoring of private investments and the related decision making process. Beside the comparison of commercial metrics e.g. revenue, cost, margin or pipeline related there shall be a variety of different KPIs that are relevant for the entire product portfolio. This equals the development of the different company management models by Donaldson Brown in 2014 that changed from the DuPont Scheme focused on the commercial KPIs only.[7]

For sure the DuPont model is still equipped with a huge variety of numbers in use for the entire company and – all the related measurements are still required but based on the change of society, the development of companies the future change of Business drove new Management and engagement Models e.g. the Balanced Scorecard.[8]

Therefore, the change in the variety of KPIs leads to a diverse set of measurement parameters inside the entire portfolio.

---

[7] Flesher, D.; Previts G.: DONALDSON BROWN (1885-1965): THE POWER OF AN INDIVIDUAL AND HIS IDEAS OVER TIME (06,2013)

[8] Kaplan, R., Norton, D.: Balanced Scorecard: Translating Strategy into Action (1996)

Portfolio management involves the management of a collection of assets with the goal of achieving specific investment objectives. KPIs are crucial metrics that help evaluate the performance of a portfolio. When evaluating comparable KPIs, it's important to consider various factors that can provide insights into the portfolio's risk, return, and overall effectiveness. Here are some key considerations:

Return Metrics:

All related commercial metrics, not limited to the ones mentioned and outlined below even more they shall contain all important commercial aspects of a product.

- Total Return: Calculates the overall performance of the portfolio, including capital gains and income.
- Annualized Return: Adjusts the total return to an annualized rate, providing a standardized measure for performance comparison.
- Relative Return: Measures the portfolio's performance relative to a benchmark index.

Risk Metrics:

A portfolio should be measured also based on the risk related implications that can occur, therefore potential implications may be measured.

- Standard Deviation: Measures the variability of returns, indicating the portfolio's volatility.
- Beta: Quantifies the portfolio's sensitivity to market movements compared to a benchmark.
- Drawdown: Evaluates the maximum loss from a peak to a trough, indicating downside risk.

Risk-Adjusted Performance Metrics:

As every product, project or solution may be in fear or connected to certain risks, there are also Risk parameters that need to be measured.

- Sharpe Ratio: Measures the excess return per unit of risk, considering the risk-free rate.
- Sortino Ratio: The Sortino ratio is a useful way for investors, analysts, and portfolio managers to evaluate an investment's return for a given level of bad risk. It only considers negative deviations. Similar to Sharpe ratio but focuses on downside risk, using the downside deviation instead of standard deviation.[9]

Diversification Metrics:

Companies are always looking how to expand their footprint in their industry, increase the revenue or grow the margin. 70% of all all large companies around the world operate in more than two industries based on McKinsey. This could be a result of diversification. Diversification is a corporate Strategy to increase market penetration through delivering value in different industries or business units. It could also mean the diversification of a portfolio to invest in different asset classes to reduce risk.[10]

- Correlation: Examines the degree to which the portfolio's assets move in relation to each other.
- Diversification Ratio: Measures the extent to which the portfolio is diversified, indicating the potential risk reduction from diversification.

---

[9] Sortino, F.: The Sortino Framework for Constructing Portfolios: Focusing on Desired Target ReturnT to Optimize Upside Potential Relative to Downside Risk (2009)
[10] Caudillo, F., Houben, S., Noor, J.: Mapping the value of diversification, McKinsey (2015)

Income and Yield Metrics:

Yield metrics play a pivotal role in portfolio management, providing valuable insights into the income generation aspect of an investment portfolio. These metrics assess the effectiveness of a portfolio in generating returns through interest, dividends, and other income sources. Investors and portfolio managers often rely on yield metrics to evaluate the income potential, assess risk-adjusted returns, and make informed decisions about asset allocation. From dividend yields to yield on cost, these metrics contribute to a comprehensive understanding of a portfolio's performance, helping investors strike a balance between capital appreciation and income generation within their investment objectives. In essence, yield metrics serve as critical tools for investors seeking to optimize their portfolio's financial performance and align their investment strategy with specific income goals.

- Yield on Cost: Calculates the current yield based on the initial cost of the investment.
- Dividend Yield: Measures the annual dividend income relative to the investment cost.

Liquidity Metrics:

Liquidity is a fundamental aspect of portfolio management, representing the ease with which assets can be bought or sold in the market without significantly impacting their prices. In the dynamic world of finance, understanding and effectively managing liquidity is essential for investors and portfolio managers alike. Liquidity metrics serve as valuable tools to gauge the level of marketability and the potential impact of trading on a portfolio's assets. From bid-ask spreads to portfolio turnover ratios, these metrics offer insights into the efficiency and cost-effectiveness of executing trades. In this intricate landscape, where quick and efficient transactions can be as crucial as investment decisions themselves, liquidity metrics play a central role in shaping and optimizing portfolio strategies. This introduction highlights the significance of liquidity and the pivotal role that liquidity metrics play in ensuring portfolios remain adaptable and responsive in various market conditions.

- Portfolio Turnover Ratio: Reflects the frequency of buying and selling within the portfolio, indicating liquidity needs.
- Bid-Ask Spread: Measures the cost of trading, considering the difference between buying and selling prices.

Concentration Metrics:

Concentration metrics in portfolio management are vital tools for assessing the degree of diversification within an investment portfolio. Concentration refers to the extent to which a portfolio is exposed to a limited number of assets, sectors, or geographic regions. In other words, it measures the level of risk associated with having a significant portion of the portfolio allocated to a small number of holdings.

Effective diversification is a key strategy to manage risk and enhance the stability of a portfolio. Concentration metrics provide insights into the distribution of assets, helping investors and portfolio managers evaluate potential vulnerabilities and identify opportunities for risk mitigation. Whether assessing the concentration of top holdings, sectors, or geographic exposures, these metrics play a crucial role in optimizing portfolio composition and aligning it with the investor's risk tolerance and overall financial objectives.

In this context, concentration metrics serve as essential instruments for achieving a balanced and resilient portfolio, ensuring that the investment strategy is well-positioned to weather market fluctuations and capitalize on diverse opportunities. This introduction underscores the importance of concentration metrics in the broader landscape of portfolio management, emphasizing their role in enhancing risk management strategies and fostering more robust investment decisions.

- Top Holdings Exposure: Assesses the concentration risk by evaluating the percentage of the portfolio invested in its top holdings.
- Sector Concentration: Examines the allocation of assets across different sectors.

Environmental, Social, and Governance (ESG) Metrics:

Environmental, Social, and Governance (ESG) considerations have emerged as integral components of modern portfolio management, reflecting a broader recognition of the impact that companies' environmental practices, social policies, and governance structures can have on their financial performance and long-term sustainability. ESG in portfolio management entails integrating these non-financial factors into the investment decision-making process to create portfolios that align with ethical, sustainable, and responsible principles. This is also one of the key trends in portfolio management [see chapter on Future Trends: ESG (Environmental, Social, and Governance) Integration].

Investors and portfolio managers are increasingly acknowledging that a company's commitment to environmental stewardship, social responsibility, and effective governance can influence its risk profile and long-term value. As a result, ESG metrics have become essential tools for evaluating the overall sustainability and ethical practices of potential investments.

This paradigm shift in portfolio management is driven by a growing awareness of the interconnectedness between corporate behavior and financial performance. Portfolios that incorporate ESG criteria aim not only for financial returns but also for positive social and environmental impact. This introduction highlights the transformative role of ESG considerations in shaping investment strategies, fostering a more conscientious approach to portfolio construction, and addressing the evolving expectations of investors who seek both financial gains and positive societal contributions.

- ESG Rating: Evaluates the portfolio's exposure to environmental, social, and governance factors (e.g. investment in sustainable technologies, total land used for operations, et. al.)
- Carbon Footprint: Measures the carbon emissions associated with the portfolio's holdings. This could even include a lot more KPIs e.g. Waste Management, Energy consumption, water consumption, et. al.
- Diversity and Inclusion: Represents the representation of different groups inside the organization.
- Employee Diversity: Measurement of different employee groups and their representation
- Social parameters: Employee satisfaction, number of incidents, percentage of women in leadership roles, et. al.

As there is a large variety of different ESG criteria, the European Federation of Financial Analysts Societies (EFFAS) has developed an ESG framework that provides guidelines for reporting KPIs.[11]

Expense Metrics:

This could be the expense ratio or comparable elements that develop the metric (Expense Ratio: Evaluates the cost efficiency of managing the portfolio).

Benchmark Metrics:

Benchmarking KPIs is a crucial practice in portfolio management, providing a means to assess the relative performance of a portfolio against a chosen standard or benchmark. KPIs serve as quantifiable measures of success, allowing investors and portfolio managers to gauge how well their investments are performing compared to an established reference point.

---

[11] European Federation of Financial Analysts Societies (EFFAS), effas.com

Benchmarking KPIs in portfolio management involves the careful selection of relevant metrics, such as return on investment, volatility, or risk-adjusted performance, and comparing these against a benchmark index or other benchmarks. This process helps investors gain insights into the portfolio's strengths and weaknesses, identify areas for improvement, and make informed decisions about asset allocation and strategy adjustments.

In a landscape where market conditions are dynamic and diverse, benchmarking KPIs provides a valuable framework for evaluating investment choices objectively. It allows investors to set realistic performance expectations, measure the effectiveness of their investment strategy, and ensure that the portfolio aligns with their financial goals. This introduction underscores the significance of benchmarking KPIs as a strategic tool in portfolio management, facilitating a data-driven approach to performance evaluation and decision-making.

- Tracking Error: Measures the deviation of the portfolio's performance from its benchmark.
- Information Ratio: Assesses the portfolio manager's ability to generate excess returns relative to the benchmark.

When evaluating comparable KPIs, it's essential to consider the investment objectives, risk tolerance, and time horizon of the portfolio. Additionally, understanding the economic and market conditions is crucial for interpreting the KPIs accurately. Regular monitoring and periodic reassessment of the portfolio's performance against these metrics can inform strategic decisions and adjustments to the investment strategy.

Review, Adaptation & Optimization:

Periodic reviews of the portfolio are conducted to assess its performance and relevance. Adjustments are made as necessary to reflect changes in the business environment or strategic priorities.

As outlined in Figure 5: Product lifecycle and corporate actions above the entire lifecycle or value chain requires continuous monitoring to identify the related need for optimization and adjustment.

Benefits of Portfolio Management

The opportunity of portfolio management offers the chance to grow on a certain level of products that interact on a certain demand, alignment or need across the entire Organization. Portfolio management offers a range of benefits to corporate enterprises:

- Strategic Alignment:

By selecting and prioritizing projects that align with the company's strategic objectives, portfolio management ensures that resources are allocated to initiatives that contribute directly to the organization's success.

- Risk Management:

Diversification within a portfolio helps spread risk. If one project encounters difficulties, the impact on the overall portfolio is minimized, reducing the organization's exposure to risk.

- Resource Optimization:

Effective portfolio management allows organizations to allocate resources efficiently. Projects with the highest strategic value receive the necessary attention and resources, leading to improved overall performance.

- Enhanced Decision-Making:

Data-driven decision-making is a hallmark of portfolio management. By relying on quantitative and qualitative analysis, organizations can make informed choices about which projects to pursue and how to allocate resources.

- Adaptability:

In a dynamic business environment, portfolio management provides a mechanism for organizations to adapt to changing circumstances. Projects can be added, removed, or reprioritized to respond to new opportunities or challenges.

Conclusion

In conclusion, portfolio management is a critical practice that helps corporate enterprises achieve their strategic objectives by optimizing resource allocation, managing risk, and fostering adaptability. Throughout this book, we will explore in greater detail the various aspects of portfolio management, including its fundamental principles, methodologies, best practices, and real-world case studies. By mastering the art of portfolio management, organizations can enhance their competitiveness and position themselves for sustained success in today's dynamic business landscape.

The Fundamentals of Corporate Portfolio Management

This chapter delves deeper into the fundamentals of portfolio management, including the definition of a portfolio, the types of portfolios commonly managed in corporate settings, and the basic principles that underpin effective portfolio management. Case studies and real-world examples will illustrate the concepts introduced, helping readers grasp their practical applications.

Defining Corporate Portfolios

A corporate portfolio consists of a collection of projects, programs, and initiatives that an organization undertakes to achieve its strategic goals. These projects can span various functions, departments, and business units within the company. It's important to differentiate between project management and portfolio management: while project management focuses on the successful execution of individual projects, portfolio management is concerned with the strategic selection, prioritization, and oversight of multiple projects to maximize value and alignment with the organization's objectives.

Types of Portfolios

Corporate portfolios come in various forms, depending on the organization's industry, size, and goals. Some common types of portfolios include:

- Project Portfolios:

These consist of a collection of individual projects aimed at delivering specific outcomes. Project portfolios are typically found in organizations with a project-centric approach, such as construction companies or consulting firms.

- Product Portfolios:

In product-based industries, organizations manage portfolios of products or product lines. These portfolios include new product development initiatives, product enhancements, and product retirements.

- Investment Portfolios:

In financial institutions and investment firms, portfolios consist of a mix of assets like stocks, bonds, and real estate. Portfolio managers aim to optimize returns while managing risk.

- Research and Development (R&D) Portfolios:

Innovation-driven companies manage R&D portfolios that encompass various research projects and product development efforts. These portfolios aim to keep the company competitive and innovative.

The Objectives of Portfolio Management

Portfolio Management is established to evaluate on details and insights about the portfolio management approach. Based on a SWOT analysis thier may be spots identified that have a direct impact on the portfolio and related path forward decision. The primary objectives of corporate portfolio management include:

- Strategic Alignment:

Ensure that the portfolio's projects and initiatives align with the organization's strategic objectives. This requires a deep understanding of the company's mission, vision, and long-term goals.

- Resource Optimization:

Allocate resources (financial, human, and technological) effectively among portfolio components to maximize value and minimize waste. This could be done by a portfolio health report to identify and execute a Benchmarking of portfolio Elements against each other. If you are looking at portfolios of the same age you may encounter that there is an R&D share to be considered.

- Performance Measurement:

Establish key performance indicators (KPIs) and metrics to monitor and evaluate portfolio performance. This helps ensure that the portfolio remains on track to achieve its objectives. Performance Measurement can relate to commercial implications but include also adoption and other success criteria related to a certain solution, product or project.

The Fundamental Principles of Portfolio Management

The ambition that is driving Portfolio Management is the continuous benchmarking & improvement cycle of all products in the portfolio to meet the long term ambitions of a company.

- Value Creation:

The core purpose of a portfolio is to create value for the organization. Value can be financial, strategic, operational, or a combination of these. Portfolio managers must continually assess how each project contributes to value creation.

- Balanced Portfolio:

A balanced portfolio comprises a mix of projects with varying risk levels and returns. Balancing the portfolio ensures that it aligns with the organization's risk tolerance and strategic goals.

- Strategic Alignment:

Every project within the portfolio should directly support the organization's strategic objectives. Regular alignment assessments help ensure that the portfolio remains on track.

- Governance:

Effective governance structures and processes are critical for portfolio management. Governance ensures accountability, transparency, and decision-making consistency throughout the portfolio's lifecycle.

The fundamentals of corporate portfolio management lay the groundwork for effective decision-making and value creation within an organization. In the following chapters, we will delve deeper into each stage of the portfolio management process, exploring methodologies, best practices, and advanced techniques that can help corporate enterprises master the art and science of portfolio management.

Establishing Portfolio Objectives and Strategic Alignment

The cornerstone of effective corporate portfolio management lies in the establishment of clear and well-defined portfolio objectives that are tightly aligned with the organization's strategic direction. Without this alignment, a portfolio may become a collection of disparate projects and initiatives lacking a unifying purpose. In this section, we will explore the critical process of defining portfolio objectives and ensuring strategic alignment.

The Importance of Portfolio Objectives

Portfolio objectives serve as the guiding principles that dictate which projects and initiatives are included in the portfolio and why. These objectives provide a framework for decision-making, resource allocation, and performance measurement. When establishing portfolio objectives, organizations should consider the following key factors:

Strategic Priorities:

Portfolio objectives must align with the organization's strategic priorities. These strategic priorities may include market expansion, cost reduction, innovation, or customer satisfaction. Portfolio managers must thoroughly understand these priorities to ensure that selected projects contribute meaningfully to achieving them.

Risk Tolerance:

Portfolio objectives should reflect the organization's risk appetite. Some portfolios may prioritize high-risk, high-reward projects, while others may emphasize stability and risk mitigation. Defining risk tolerance helps in selecting projects that match the organization's risk profile.

Resource Constraints:

Resource availability and constraints play a crucial role in shaping portfolio objectives. Organizations must consider their financial, human, and technological resources when setting objectives to ensure they are realistic and achievable.

The Process of Establishing Portfolio Objectives

Defining portfolio objectives is not a one-size-fits-all process; it requires a systematic approach tailored to the organization's unique circumstances. The following steps can guide organizations in this process:

Reviewing the Strategic Plan:

Begin by reviewing the organization's strategic plan and identifying the key goals and priorities outlined in it. This serves as the foundation for establishing portfolio objectives.

Stakeholder Engagement:

Engage key stakeholders, including senior leadership, department heads, and project managers, in discussions about portfolio objectives. Their insights and perspectives are invaluable in ensuring alignment with strategic goals.

Defining Objectives:

With a comprehensive understanding of the strategic plan and input from stakeholders, define clear and measurable portfolio objectives. These objectives should be specific, achievable, relevant, and time-bound (SMART).

Prioritization:

In cases where multiple objectives compete for resources, prioritize them based on their strategic importance and potential impact on the organization. This prioritization ensures that the most critical objectives receive the necessary attention.

Documentation:

Document the established portfolio objectives in a clear and accessible manner. This documentation serves as a reference point for portfolio managers, project teams, and stakeholders throughout the portfolio's lifecycle.

Ensuring Strategic Alignment

Strategic alignment is the process of ensuring that every project and initiative within the portfolio directly contributes to the organization's strategic objectives. Achieving strategic alignment requires ongoing vigilance and careful evaluation. Here's how organizations can ensure strategic alignment:

- Regular Assessment:

Periodically assess each project's alignment with the established portfolio objectives and the organization's strategic plan. This assessment may involve key performance indicators (KPIs) and a review of project progress.

- Adjustments:

If a project's alignment wanes or if strategic priorities shift, be prepared to make adjustments. This may involve reprioritizing projects, reallocating resources, or even discontinuing initiatives that no longer align.

- Communication:

Effective communication is paramount in maintaining strategic alignment. Ensure that all stakeholders understand how their projects fit into the larger portfolio and contribute to the organization's overarching strategy.

Establishing portfolio objectives and ensuring strategic alignment are pivotal steps in the corporate portfolio management process. When done effectively, these processes enable organizations to focus their resources on projects that directly contribute to strategic success, enhance adaptability to changing market conditions, and maximize the value generated by their portfolios. In the chapters that follow, we will delve into the practical methodologies and tools that support these foundational principles.

The portfolio selection process is a sophisticated endeavor that goes beyond mere asset allocation and risk management. It demands a deep appreciation for the strategic alignment between investment objectives, risk tolerance, and the dynamic nature of financial markets.

The best approach to achieve Success Through Strategic Alignment in Portfolio Selection

Strategic alignment in portfolio selection involves harmonizing investment objectives with the chosen investment strategy and risk management framework. It requires a careful examination of the investor's goals, time horizon, and risk tolerance to ensure that the portfolio's composition aligns seamlessly with these fundamental considerations. Strategic alignment acts as a guiding principle, shaping every decision made throughout the portfolio construction and management process.

One of the first steps in achieving strategic alignment is tailoring asset allocation to specific investment objectives. Whether the goal is capital appreciation, income generation, or a balanced approach, the allocation of assets across different classes should be meticulously crafted to reflect these objectives. A strategic alignment ensures that the portfolio's composition is purposefully designed to meet the investor's financial aspirations.

Strategic alignment recognizes the dynamic nature of financial markets and necessitates a proactive approach to asset allocation. While adhering to a strategic framework, investors must also be prepared to make adjustments based on evolving market conditions, economic trends, and geopolitical factors. This dynamic asset allocation strategy ensures that the portfolio remains resilient and responsive to changing circumstances, maintaining strategic alignment over time.

Strategic alignment extends to risk management, where the investor's risk tolerance is carefully considered. The chosen risk management strategy should be in harmony with the investor's comfort level with market fluctuations. Strategic alignment ensures that the risk profile of the portfolio is not only aligned with the investor's tolerance but also calibrated to optimize returns within the accepted risk parameters.

Benchmarking becomes a strategic tool in evaluating the performance of a portfolio. By selecting benchmarks that align with the chosen investment strategy and objectives, investors gain a comprehensive understanding of how well their portfolio is performing relative to established standards. This strategic benchmarking provides valuable insights for ongoing assessment and potential adjustments to maintain strategic alignment.

In the contemporary investment landscape, the integration of Environmental, Social, and Governance (ESG) considerations exemplifies strategic alignment. Investors who incorporate ESG factors into their portfolio selection process not only contribute to ethical and sustainable practices but also align their investments with broader societal values, enhancing the long-term strategic outlook of the portfolio.

Strategic alignment serves as a guiding principle that permeates every facet of the portfolio selection process. It involves a holistic understanding of the investor's objectives, a dynamic approach to asset allocation and risk management, and a commitment to ethical and sustainable practices. This alignment positions the portfolio for success, fostering adaptability, resilience, and the ability to navigate the complexities of financial markets with a clear and purposeful strategy.

Achieving success in the portfolio selection process hinges on strategic alignment. Investors who carefully align their investment objectives, risk tolerance, and strategies create portfolios that are not only well-constructed but also adaptable to the evolving dynamics of the financial landscape. Strategic alignment, therefore, emerges as a cornerstone in the pursuit of investment success, guiding investors towards portfolios that not only meet financial aspirations but also reflect a thoughtful and purposeful approach to wealth management.

Portfolio Selection and Prioritization

This chapter delves into the critical processes of selecting and prioritizing projects and investments within a portfolio. Readers will explore various methods and models for evaluating potential projects, weighing their strategic importance, and allocating resources effectively. Case studies and best practices from leading corporate enterprises will offer valuable insights.

Portfolio selection and prioritization are fundamental processes in portfolio management. These activities are crucial for organizations seeking to allocate resources effectively, minimize risk, and ensure alignment with strategic objectives. In this comprehensive essay, we will explore the concepts, methodologies, and best practices involved in portfolio selection and prioritization.

The portfolio selection process is a nuanced and multifaceted journey that lies at the heart of successful investment management. Investors navigate a dynamic and complex financial landscape, where strategic decision-making is crucial for achieving financial goals while managing risk. This essay explores the intricate process of portfolio selection, unraveling its key components and emphasizing the interplay between art and science in constructing well-balanced and resilient investment portfolios.

The foundation of the portfolio selection process begins with a clear definition of investment objectives. Investors must articulate their financial goals, risk tolerance, and time horizon. Whether seeking capital appreciation, income generation, or a balance of both, a precise understanding of objectives lays the groundwork for subsequent decisions.

Asset allocation, often referred to as the cornerstone of portfolio construction, involves deciding how to distribute investments across various asset classes. Modern Portfolio Theory (MPT) plays a pivotal role in guiding these decisions, emphasizing the importance of diversification to optimize returns for a given level of risk. Investors must choose between strategic, tactical, or dynamic asset allocation strategies based on their investment horizon and market outlook.

Understanding Portfolio Selection

Portfolio selection involves the strategic process of choosing the right mix of projects, programs, and initiatives that will collectively contribute to an organization's strategic goals. It is a complex decision-making exercise that requires careful consideration of various factors, including project viability, resource availability, risk exposure, and alignment with the organization's mission and vision.

1. Strategic Alignment

The foundation of portfolio selection is strategic alignment. Every project or initiative under consideration should directly contribute to the organization's strategic objectives. It requires a deep understanding of the organization's goals, priorities, and market positioning.

2. Market Analytics and implications

Informed decision-making relies on robust market analysis and research. Investors employ fundamental and technical analyses to evaluate the financial health of individual securities and assess broader market trends. Macro-economic factors, geopolitical events, and industry-specific dynamics all contribute to the intricate tapestry of information that shapes investment decisions.

3. Risk Assessment

Risk is inherent in any portfolio. Effective portfolio selection involves assessing the risk associated with each project and evaluating how those risks align with the organization's risk tolerance. Some projects may carry high risks but offer significant rewards, while others may be lower risk but with more modest returns.

4. Resource Allocation

Resource allocation is a critical consideration in portfolio selection. Organizations must assess their available resources, including financial, human, and technological, and ensure that they can support the selected portfolio of projects. Balancing resource constraints with strategic objectives is a key challenge.

5. ESG Considerations:

In the contemporary landscape, Environmental, Social, and Governance (ESG) considerations have gained prominence. Investors increasingly recognize the impact of a company's sustainable practices on long-term financial performance. Integrating ESG criteria into the portfolio selection process allows investors to align their investments with ethical and responsible principles.

6. Implementation strategies

The choice between active and passive investing, stock picking versus index investing, and the emergence of robo-advisors and algorithmic trading are crucial elements of the implementation phase. Each strategy carries its own set of advantages and considerations, requiring investors to align their approach with their risk tolerance and investment goals.

7. Portfolio Optimization

Optimization aims to achieve the best possible combination of projects within the constraints of available resources and risk tolerance. It involves selecting projects that collectively maximize value and strategic alignment while minimizing risk.

The portfolio selection process is a dynamic and intricate journey that demands a delicate balance between the art of intuition and the science of analysis. Investors who embark on this journey armed with a clear understanding of their objectives, a strategic approach to asset allocation, and a commitment to ongoing research and monitoring are better positioned to navigate the complexities of the financial markets. As the investment landscape continues to evolve, the portfolio selection process remains an adaptive and essential tool for achieving financial success.

Methodologies for Portfolio Selection

Several methodologies can assist organizations in portfolio selection as a portfolio does not always depend on commercial data and may have a variety of numbers that are relevant for the business to execute the process from an E2E perspective. This might reflect in legal information / new jurisdictions.

1. Scoring Models

Scoring models assign scores to each project based on predefined criteria, such as strategic alignment, potential ROI, risk level, and resource requirements. Projects with the highest scores are selected for the portfolio.

2. Weighted Scoring Models

Weighted scoring models assign different weights to each criterion based on their importance to the organization's strategy. This approach allows for a more nuanced evaluation of projects.

3. Benefit-Cost Analysis

Benefit-cost analysis involves comparing the expected benefits (such as revenue generation or cost reduction) to the costs associated with each project. Projects with a favorable benefit-cost ratio are prioritized.

4. Risk Assessment Models

Risk assessment models evaluate the potential risks associated with each project and assess their impact on the portfolio. Projects with lower-risk profiles may receive higher priority.

Prioritization within the Portfolio

Once projects are selected for the portfolio, prioritization becomes essential for effective resource allocation and execution. Prioritization helps determine the order in which projects are executed, taking into account their strategic importance, dependencies, and resource availability.

1. Strategic Priority

Projects aligned with the organization's top strategic priorities are typically given the highest priority. These are the projects that have the most significant impact on achieving strategic objectives.

2. Resource Availability

Resource constraints often dictate project prioritization. Projects that can be executed with existing resources or minimal additional investment may be prioritized to optimize resource utilization.

3. Dependencies

Projects with interdependencies may need to be prioritized based on their dependencies. Projects that must precede others or have critical dependencies may take precedence.

4. Time Sensitivity

Projects with time-sensitive components, such as regulatory compliance or market opportunities, may need to be prioritized to ensure that deadlines are met.

5. Risk Management

Prioritization can also consider risk management. Lower-risk projects may be prioritized initially to build confidence in the portfolio, while higher-risk projects are carefully monitored and executed later.

Challenges in Portfolio Selection and Prioritization

While portfolio selection and prioritization offer substantial benefits, they come with challenges:

1. Data Availability and Accuracy

Accurate data on project performance, resource availability, and market conditions are crucial for effective selection and prioritization. Organizations may struggle to obtain and maintain reliable data.

2. Dynamic Business Environment

The dynamic nature of the business environment means that organizations must continually reassess and adjust their portfolios to remain competitive. This demands flexibility and adaptability in selection and prioritization.

3. Conflicting Stakeholder Interests

Stakeholders with different priorities and interests may advocate for the inclusion or prioritization of specific projects. Balancing these conflicting interests can be challenging.

4. Limited Resources

Resource constraints can limit the number and scale of projects that can be included in the portfolio. Effective prioritization is essential to optimize resource utilization.

5. Risk Management

Effective risk assessment and mitigation strategies are essential but can be complex and time-consuming.

Portfolio selection and prioritization are core processes in portfolio management that drive strategic success. They require organizations to align projects with their strategic objectives, assess risks, allocate resources effectively, and make informed decisions. By adopting appropriate methodologies and best practices, organizations can navigate the challenges and complexities of portfolio selection and prioritization, ultimately achieving their strategic goals and maximizing the value of their portfolios.

Risk Management in Portfolio Management

Risk is an inherent part of portfolio management, and this chapter will cover techniques for identifying, assessing, and mitigating risks within corporate portfolios. Readers will gain an understanding of how risk factors into decision-making and learn how to develop risk management strategies that safeguard the achievement of portfolio objectives.

The generic definition of risk as "any uncertainty that, if it occurs, will affect achievement of objectives" allows us to define any level of risk that interferes with our companies' objectives.

Risk management is a critical component of portfolio management in corporate enterprises. It is the process of identifying, assessing, and mitigating risks to protect and enhance the value of the portfolio. In this essay, we will explore the multifaceted role of risk management in portfolio management, its key principles, methodologies, and its crucial importance in achieving strategic success.

Understanding Risk in Portfolio Management

Risk, in the context of portfolio management, refers to the potential for adverse outcomes that can affect the achievement of portfolio objectives. These adverse outcomes can take various forms, including financial losses, project delays, resource constraints, and strategic misalignment. Risks can emanate from internal factors, such as project execution issues, or external factors, such as market fluctuations, regulatory changes, or natural disasters.

The Objectives of Risk Management in Portfolio Management

Preserving Value: The primary objective of risk management is to protect the value of the portfolio. By identifying and mitigating risks, portfolio managers aim to prevent losses and safeguard the investments made in various projects and initiatives.

Optimizing Risk-Reward Trade-Off: Portfolio managers seek to strike a balance between risk and reward. They aim to optimize the portfolio's risk-return profile, ensuring that the expected benefits justify the inherent risks.

Enhancing Decision-Making: Risk management provides decision-makers with valuable information to make informed choices. It allows them to assess the impact of risks on portfolio objectives and make adjustments as necessary.

Adaptability: An effective risk management framework equips organizations with the flexibility to adapt to changing circumstances. It helps identify emerging risks and devise strategies to address them promptly.

Key Principles of Risk Management in Portfolio Management

Risk Identification: The first step in risk management is identifying potential risks. This involves examining all aspects of the portfolio, including individual projects, and recognizing factors that could pose a threat to the portfolio's objectives.

Risk Assessment: Once risks are identified, they need to be assessed. This involves estimating the likelihood of each risk occurring and the potential impact it could have on the portfolio. This assessment is often performed quantitatively and qualitatively.

Risk Mitigation: After assessing risks, portfolio managers develop strategies to mitigate them. These strategies can include risk avoidance, risk transfer, risk reduction, or risk acceptance. The choice of strategy depends on the risk's severity and the organization's risk tolerance.

Continuous Monitoring: Risk management is an ongoing process. Portfolio managers must continuously monitor the portfolio and its constituent projects for new risks and changes in the risk landscape. Regular reviews help ensure that risk mitigation strategies remain effective.

Integration with Strategic Objectives: Effective risk management aligns with the portfolio's strategic objectives. This means that risks are assessed not only in terms of their financial impact but also their potential to derail strategic initiatives.

Methodologies and Tools for Risk Management

Risk Registers: A risk register is a structured document that catalogs identified risks, their potential impacts, and mitigation strategies. It serves as a central reference point for portfolio managers and stakeholders.

Probability-Impact Matrices: These matrices help in prioritizing risks by plotting them on a matrix based on their probability and impact. High-probability, high-impact risks are typically addressed with greater urgency.

Monte Carlo Simulation: This statistical technique allows portfolio managers to model the impact of various risks on the portfolio's performance. It provides a probabilistic view of potential outcomes, helping in risk assessment.

Sensitivity Analysis: Sensitivity analysis examines how changes in specific variables or risks can affect the portfolio's performance. It helps identify which risks have the most significant impact.

Key Risk Indicators (KRIs): KRIs are quantifiable metrics used to monitor specific risks. They provide early warning signals, allowing for timely risk response.

The Role of Technology in Risk Management

Technology plays a vital role in modern risk management within portfolio management. Portfolio management software and data analytics tools enable organizations to:

- Automate risk identification and assessment processes.
- Perform real-time monitoring of portfolio performance against predefined risk thresholds.
- Utilize big data analytics to identify emerging risks and trends.
- Facilitate collaboration and communication among stakeholders involved in risk management.
- Conclusion

In today's volatile business environment, risk management is not an option but a necessity for corporate portfolio management. By systematically identifying, assessing, and mitigating risks, organizations can protect their investments, optimize their portfolios, and enhance decision-making. Risk management is not a static process; it evolves as the portfolio landscape changes. Hence, it's crucial for portfolio managers to continually adapt and refine their risk management strategies to navigate uncertainty and achieve strategic success.

Portfolio Optimization and Performance Measurement

This chapter focuses on the optimization of corporate portfolios to maximize returns and achieve strategic objectives. It will introduce optimization models and methodologies and guide readers through the process of continually monitoring and measuring portfolio performance. Key performance indicators (KPIs) and metrics will be discussed, along with strategies for adapting portfolios in response to changing circumstances.

Portfolio optimization and performance measurement are critical aspects of corporate portfolio management. Optimization involves the strategic allocation of resources to maximize returns and achieve portfolio objectives, while performance measurement assesses the effectiveness of these decisions. In this comprehensive chapter, we will delve into the principles, methodologies, and practical strategies for portfolio optimization and performance measurement.

Portfolio Optimization

- The Goal of Portfolio Optimization

Portfolio optimization aims to strike the right balance between risk and return. It involves selecting the optimal combination of projects, programs, and initiatives within the portfolio to achieve the organization's strategic objectives while considering resource constraints, risk tolerance, and market dynamics.

- Risk and Return Trade-Off

Central to portfolio optimization is the concept of the risk-return trade-off. Higher returns often come with higher risks, and portfolio managers must assess and manage this trade-off carefully. The risk-return profile should align with the organization's risk appetite and strategic goals.

- Asset Allocation

Asset allocation is a fundamental component of portfolio optimization. It involves deciding how to distribute resources among various projects and initiatives. Modern portfolio theory, developed by Harry Markowitz, plays a significant role in asset allocation. Markowitz's theory highlights the importance of diversification in reducing risk.

Portfolio Optimization Models

Several mathematical models and techniques are used for portfolio optimization, including:

Mean-Variance Optimization: This classic approach minimizes risk for a given level of return or maximizes return for a given level of risk. It considers the expected returns and variances of individual assets within the portfolio.

Capital Market Line (CML) and Efficient Frontier: These graphical tools help visualize the risk-return trade-off and identify portfolios that offer the best risk-adjusted returns.

Monte Carlo Simulation: Monte Carlo simulations model the impact of different variables and risks on portfolio performance, allowing for more realistic optimization scenarios.

Performance Measurement

The general imperative for Performance Measurement raised from the DuPont scheme to the Balanced Scorecard but for Portfolio related Measurement it is key to define correlated strategies how to execute on the portfolio. Performance measurement provides a means of evaluating the effectiveness of portfolio management decisions and strategies. It helps answer essential questions, such as whether the portfolio is on track to meet its objectives, whether resources are allocated efficiently, and how well risks are being managed.

Key Performance Indicators (KPIs)

Key performance indicators are essential metrics used to assess portfolio performance. Common KPIs in portfolio management include:

- Return on Investment (ROI): Measures the profitability of the portfolio.
- Risk-Adjusted Return (Sharpe Ratio): Evaluates returns relative to the level of risk taken.
- Portfolio Volatility: Measures the variability of portfolio returns.
- Tracking Error: Assesses how closely the portfolio follows its benchmark index.
- Portfolio Turnover: Measures how frequently assets are bought and sold within the portfolio.

Benchmarking

Benchmarking involves comparing the portfolio's performance to a relevant benchmark, such as a market index or peer group. This helps assess how well the portfolio is performing relative to its peers and whether it is meeting its objectives. Benchmarking can be done with other similar products, projects or portfolios but even more it could also be executed as cross organizational Benchmark for Organizations and companies in similar or different sectors.

Benchmarks serve as yardsticks that facilitate a comparative analysis of a portfolio's performance. They provide a standard against which investors can measure returns, assess risk, and gauge the effectiveness of their investment strategies. In essence, benchmarks play a pivotal role in shaping the goals and expectations within the portfolio management framework.

Choosing the right benchmark is a critical decision in the portfolio management process. A well-selected benchmark aligns with the investment objectives and asset allocation strategy of the portfolio. Investors may opt for broad market indices, sector-specific benchmarks, or custom benchmarks that closely resemble the composition of their portfolios. The appropriateness of the benchmark ensures a meaningful evaluation of the portfolio's relative performance.

Benchmarking involves the comparison of portfolio performance against predetermined KPIs. Common KPIs include total return, standard deviation, and risk-adjusted ratios such as the Sharpe ratio or Information ratio. These metrics provide nuanced insights into the portfolio's risk and return profile, enabling investors to assess whether their strategies are delivering value in comparison to the benchmark.

Effective risk management is a cornerstone of portfolio management, and benchmarks serve as valuable tools in this regard. Benchmarks provide a basis for evaluating the risk-adjusted returns of a portfolio, allowing investors to identify outliers and potential sources of excess risk. This risk-aware approach contributes to a more resilient and balanced portfolio.

Periodic benchmarking reviews offer opportunities for strategic adjustments. As market conditions change and economic landscapes evolve, comparing portfolio performance against benchmarks facilitates a data-driven decision-making process. Investors can identify areas for improvement, reassess asset allocation, and make informed strategic adjustments to ensure the portfolio remains aligned with their objectives.

Diversification is a key risk mitigation strategy in portfolio management. Benchmarks aid in assessing the effectiveness of diversification by providing insights into the correlation between the portfolio and its benchmark. A well-diversified portfolio should exhibit a balance between risk and return, and benchmarking helps investors gauge the success of their diversification efforts.

While benchmarking is a powerful tool, it comes with its own set of challenges. Choosing an inappropriate benchmark or relying solely on historical performance can lead to misleading conclusions. Moreover, market conditions and economic factors can impact benchmark performance, necessitating a nuanced interpretation of results.

The symbiotic relationship between portfolio management and benchmarking underscores the importance of a systematic and data-driven approach to investment decisions. Benchmarks provide a meaningful reference point for evaluating performance, managing risk, and making strategic adjustments. Through the lens of benchmarking, portfolio management becomes a dynamic process, where investors continually refine their strategies to achieve optimal returns within acceptable risk parameters. As financial markets evolve, the integration of benchmarking practices remains essential for informed and strategic portfolio management.

Attribution Analysis

Attribution analysis breaks down portfolio performance into its constituent parts to understand the sources of returns and risks. It helps identify which assets or strategies are contributing the most to the portfolio's performance.

Practical Strategies for Portfolio Optimization and Performance Measurement

The challenge that a lot of companies have is the adjustment of the portfolio to future needs and decide if they want to expand and diversify accordingly.

Diversification

Diversification is a key strategy in portfolio optimization. By spreading investments across different assets, industries, and geographic regions, portfolio managers can reduce risk without sacrificing returns.

Rebalancing

Regular portfolio rebalancing is essential to maintain the desired asset allocation. Rebalancing ensures that the portfolio remains aligned with its objectives and risk tolerance, especially as market conditions change.

Continuous Monitoring

Continuous monitoring of portfolio performance and market conditions is crucial. It allows for timely adjustments to the portfolio's composition and strategies in response to changing circumstances.

Scenario Analysis

Scenario analysis involves evaluating how the portfolio would perform under different economic, market, or industry conditions. It helps portfolio managers assess the resilience of their strategies.

Conclusion

Portfolio optimization and performance measurement are indispensable tools for corporate portfolio managers seeking to make informed decisions, achieve strategic objectives, and navigate the complex landscape of risk and return. By understanding the principles, employing the right methodologies, and implementing practical strategies, organizations can optimize their portfolios for success in an ever-evolving business environment.

Portfolio Governance

Governance and Stakeholder Management

Effective governance is crucial in managing corporate portfolios. This chapter will explore the governance structures and processes needed to oversee portfolio management, as well as strategies for engaging stakeholders and ensuring transparency and accountability.

Effective governance and stakeholder management are essential components of successful portfolio management in corporate enterprises. In this comprehensive chapter, we will explore the critical role of governance in portfolio management, the importance of stakeholder engagement, and best practices for achieving transparency, accountability, and alignment with strategic objectives.

Governance in Portfolio Management

Governance in portfolio management refers to the establishment of structures, processes, and policies that guide decision-making, ensure accountability, and promote transparency throughout the portfolio's lifecycle. It provides the framework within which portfolio managers operate, ensuring that resources are allocated effectively and that the portfolio aligns with the organization's strategic goals.

Key Elements of Governance

Effective governance in portfolio management includes the following elements:

Clear Roles and Responsibilities: Defined roles and responsibilities for portfolio managers, steering committees, and stakeholders help avoid confusion and foster accountability.

Decision-Making Framework: A well-defined decision-making process outlines how project and portfolio decisions are made, including criteria, thresholds, and escalation procedures.

Performance Measurement and Reporting: Governance structures should establish KPIs and reporting mechanisms to assess portfolio performance and communicate results to stakeholders.

Risk Management and Compliance: Governance frameworks should include risk management processes and mechanisms to ensure compliance with regulations, standards, and policies.

Stakeholder Management

Stakeholders in portfolio management include senior executives, project managers, employees, investors, customers, and regulatory bodies. Engaging these stakeholders is crucial because they have a vested interest in the portfolio's success. Effective stakeholder management ensures that their concerns are considered, and their expectations are met.

Stakeholder Analysis

Stakeholder analysis involves identifying and categorizing stakeholders based on their influence and interest in the portfolio. This analysis helps prioritize stakeholder engagement efforts and tailor communication strategies accordingly.

Communication Strategies

Effective communication with stakeholders is key to successful portfolio management. Tailoring communication to stakeholders' needs, providing regular updates, and addressing concerns promptly fosters trust and alignment.

Conflict Resolution

Inevitably, conflicts may arise among stakeholders with differing interests. Portfolio managers must be equipped with conflict resolution strategies to address disputes and maintain stakeholder buy-in.

Best Practices for Governance and Stakeholder Management

Develop a comprehensive governance framework that defines roles, responsibilities, and decision-making processes.

Formulate governance policies that align with the organization's strategic objectives and risk tolerance.

Establish clear reporting structures to ensure that information flows efficiently between portfolio managers, decision-makers, and stakeholders.

Engaging Stakeholders

- Conduct regular stakeholder engagement sessions to gather input, address concerns, and align expectations.
- Customize communication plans for different stakeholder groups, ensuring that messages are clear, relevant, and timely.
- Utilize technology and collaboration tools to facilitate stakeholder engagement and information sharing.

Monitoring and Accountability

- Implement performance measurement mechanisms, including KPIs and dashboards, to track portfolio progress and outcomes.
- Conduct regular audits and reviews to assess compliance with governance policies and identify areas for improvement.
- Establish a culture of accountability where portfolio managers take ownership of their decisions and outcomes.

Governance and stakeholder management are cornerstones of effective portfolio management in corporate enterprises. A well-defined governance framework provides the structure for decision-making, risk management, and compliance, while stakeholder engagement ensures alignment with organizational objectives and fosters trust and support. By implementing best practices in governance and stakeholder management, organizations can enhance transparency, accountability, and ultimately, the success of their portfolios.

Portfolio Management Tools and Technologies

Readers will be introduced to the various tools and technologies available for supporting portfolio management in corporate enterprises. This chapter will cover software solutions, analytics platforms, and emerging technologies that can streamline portfolio management processes and enhance decision-making.

In today's fast-paced and dynamic business environment, portfolio management has become increasingly complex, requiring sophisticated tools and technologies to support decision-making, optimize resource allocation, and ensure alignment with strategic objectives. This essay explores the pivotal role of portfolio management tools and technologies, delves into the various categories and features of these tools, and highlights their significance in achieving strategic success.

The Evolving Landscape of Portfolio Management

Portfolio management in corporate enterprises encompasses the strategic selection, prioritization, and oversight of a collection of projects, programs, and initiatives. The goal is to maximize value, minimize risk, and ensure alignment with the organization's strategic objectives. The complexity and scale of portfolio management have expanded significantly in recent years due to factors such as globalization, technological advancements, and the need for greater agility.

The Role of Portfolio Management Tools and Technologies

Portfolio management tools and technologies play a central role in streamlining and enhancing the portfolio management process. They offer several key benefits:

Data Integration and Analysis: Portfolio management tools can aggregate data from various sources, providing a comprehensive view of projects, resources, budgets, and risks. Advanced analytics capabilities enable portfolio managers to make data-driven decisions.

Resource Allocation: These tools facilitate efficient resource allocation by helping organizations match project requirements with available resources, ensuring optimal utilization and preventing resource bottlenecks.

Risk Management: Portfolio management tools incorporate risk assessment and modeling features, allowing organizations to identify, assess, and mitigate risks effectively. Scenario analysis and Monte Carlo simulations enable proactive risk management.

Strategic Alignment: Tools and technologies help ensure that every project and initiative within the portfolio aligns with the organization's strategic objectives. They provide mechanisms for tracking alignment and making adjustments as needed.

Communication and Collaboration: Modern portfolio management tools promote collaboration among stakeholders, enabling effective communication, document sharing, and workflow management. This fosters transparency and alignment.

Categories of Portfolio Management Tools and Technologies

Portfolio management tools and technologies can be categorized into several broad groups:

Project and Portfolio Management (PPM) Software: PPM software is designed specifically for managing portfolios of projects and initiatives. It offers features for project planning, scheduling, resource allocation, and performance tracking. Examples include Microsoft Project, Oracle Primavera, and Smartsheet.

Enterprise Project Management (EPM) Systems: EPM systems extend the capabilities of PPM software to encompass broader enterprise functions. They integrate project and portfolio management with financial management, resource management, and other enterprise-level processes.

Data Analytics and Business Intelligence (BI) Tools: These tools provide advanced analytics and reporting capabilities, allowing organizations to extract insights from portfolio data. BI platforms like Tableau, QlikView, and Power BI can be integrated with portfolio management systems for enhanced reporting.

Collaboration and Workflow Tools: Collaboration platforms like Microsoft Teams, Slack, and Trello facilitate communication, document sharing, and task management among portfolio stakeholders. Integration with portfolio management systems ensures seamless collaboration.

Cloud-Based Solutions: Cloud-based portfolio management solutions offer scalability, flexibility, and accessibility. They allow organizations to manage portfolios from anywhere, and they often come with built-in security and data backup features.

Artificial Intelligence (AI) and Machine Learning (ML): AI and ML technologies are increasingly being used in portfolio management to automate routine tasks, predict project outcomes, and identify patterns and trends in data.

The Significance of Emerging Technologies

Emerging technologies are reshaping portfolio management in profound ways. For example:

Blockchain: Blockchain technology can enhance the transparency and security of portfolio data, making it tamper-proof and verifiable.

Big Data and Predictive Analytics: Big data analytics and predictive modeling enable organizations to proactively identify risks and opportunities, aiding portfolio optimization.

Robotic Process Automation (RPA): RPA can automate repetitive tasks in portfolio management, reducing manual effort and minimizing errors.

Challenges and Considerations

While portfolio management tools and technologies offer numerous advantages, their implementation comes with challenges:

- Integration Complexity: Integrating portfolio management tools with existing systems and data sources can be complex and time-consuming.
- Data Security and Privacy: Handling sensitive portfolio data requires robust security measures and compliance with data privacy regulations like GDPR.
- User Adoption: Ensuring that stakeholders effectively use these tools may require training and change management efforts.

Portfolio management tools and technologies have become indispensable in the modern corporate landscape. They empower organizations to make informed decisions, optimize resources, manage risks, and achieve strategic alignment. As technology continues to advance, organizations that leverage these tools effectively will be better positioned to navigate the complexities of portfolio management and drive strategic success in an increasingly competitive and dynamic business environment.

Future Trends and Challenges in Corporate Portfolio Management

The final chapter will explore emerging trends, challenges, and opportunities in the field of corporate portfolio management. It will provide readers with insights into how portfolio management is evolving in response to changing business landscapes and technologies and offer guidance on how to stay ahead in this dynamic field.

Corporate portfolio management is a dynamic discipline that continually evolves to meet the changing needs and challenges of today's business landscape. As organizations strive for competitiveness, growth, and innovation, portfolio management plays a pivotal role in shaping their strategic direction. In this essay, we will explore the future trends and challenges that are expected to shape corporate portfolio management in the years to come.

Trends in Corporate Portfolio Management

Digital Transformation and Technology Integration

Trend: The rapid advancement of technology, including artificial intelligence (AI), machine learning (ML), and data analytics, is transforming corporate portfolio management. Organizations are increasingly integrating digital tools to enhance decision-making, automate routine tasks, and gain insights from data.

Impact: Digital transformation enables more sophisticated risk analysis, real-time monitoring, and predictive modeling in portfolio management. It streamlines processes, reduces manual effort, and improves agility, allowing organizations to respond to market changes faster.

ESG (Environmental, Social, and Governance) Integration

Trend: Sustainability and ESG considerations are becoming central to portfolio management. Investors and stakeholders are demanding greater transparency and accountability in how companies manage their environmental and social impacts.

Impact: ESG integration requires organizations to assess the environmental and social risks and opportunities associated with their portfolio projects. Companies that effectively incorporate ESG factors can attract responsible investors and enhance their brand reputation.

Agile Portfolio Management

Trend: Agile methodologies, which originated in software development, are expanding into portfolio management. Agile portfolio management promotes adaptability, collaboration, and customer-centricity, allowing organizations to respond to changing market dynamics more effectively.

Impact: Agile portfolio management fosters quicker decision-making, iterative planning, and the ability to pivot in response to market shifts. It enhances alignment between project teams and business objectives, ultimately driving innovation and value.

Integration of Sustainability Goals

Trend: Sustainability goals are becoming integral to portfolio management. Organizations are aligning their portfolios with long-term sustainability objectives, such as carbon neutrality, renewable energy adoption, and waste reduction.

Impact: Integrating sustainability goals can result in portfolios that are both environmentally responsible and financially viable. It may require changes in project selection, resource allocation, and risk assessment to meet sustainability targets.

Greater Emphasis on Data Security and Privacy

Trend: As organizations rely more on data-driven decision-making in portfolio management, data security and privacy have become paramount. New regulations like GDPR (General Data Protection Regulation) and evolving cyber threats demand enhanced data protection measures.

Impact: Organizations must invest in robust cybersecurity measures, data encryption, and compliance frameworks to safeguard sensitive portfolio data. A breach can have severe consequences, including legal and reputational damage.

Challenges in Corporate Portfolio Management

1. Complexity and Scalability

Challenge: As portfolios expand to include a greater number of projects, programs, and initiatives, managing their complexity becomes increasingly challenging. Scalability issues can arise in resource allocation, risk assessment, and decision-making.

Mitigation: Implementing advanced portfolio management tools and methodologies can help streamline and automate processes, making it easier to manage larger and more complex portfolios.

2. Resource Constraints

Challenge: Resource constraints, including financial, human, and technological resources, can hinder portfolio optimization. Balancing resource allocation across multiple projects while meeting strategic objectives is a perennial challenge.

Mitigation: Advanced resource management tools and effective prioritization based on strategic alignment can help optimize resource allocation and address resource constraints.

3. Change Management

Challenge: Transitioning to new portfolio management methodologies or integrating digital tools often faces resistance within organizations. Change management hurdles can impede the adoption of more efficient and innovative portfolio management practices.

Mitigation: A robust change management strategy that includes training, communication, and stakeholder engagement is crucial to successfully implementing changes in portfolio management practices.

4. Data Privacy and Compliance

Challenge: Ensuring data privacy and compliance with evolving regulations is a growing challenge, particularly in a global context where data privacy laws vary.

Mitigation: Employing data encryption, access controls, and compliance frameworks, and staying informed about regulatory changes are essential measures for addressing this challenge.

5. Risk Management in a Dynamic Environment

Challenge: The business environment is becoming increasingly dynamic, with emerging risks such as cybersecurity threats, geopolitical instability, and pandemic-related disruptions. Traditional risk management approaches may not be sufficient to address these evolving risks.

Mitigation: Organizations must adopt a proactive approach to risk management, utilizing advanced risk assessment tools, scenario planning, and crisis management strategies to respond effectively to unforeseen challenges.

Corporate portfolio management is evolving in response to the digital age, sustainability imperatives, and the need for agility in a rapidly changing business landscape. While these trends bring opportunities for enhanced decision-making and value creation, they also present challenges in terms of complexity, resource allocation, change management, and risk mitigation. Addressing these challenges and leveraging the emerging trends will be crucial for organizations seeking to excel in portfolio management and achieve strategic success in the future.

Abbreviations

BSC	Balanced Scorecard
ESG	Environmental, Social & Governance
KPI	Key performance Indicator
SWOT	Strength, Weaknesses, Opportunities, Threats
PESTLE	Political, Social, Legal, Environmental, Technological, Economical
MCDM	Multi Criteria Decision Making

Table of Figures

Disclaimer:

The author generated this text in part with GPT-3, OpenAI's large-scale language-generation model. Upon generating draft language, the author reviewed, edited, and revised the language to their own liking and takes ultimate responsibility for the content of this publication.

www.ingramcontent.com/pod-product-compliance
Lightning Source LLC
Chambersburg PA
CBHW060005300526
45794CB00003B/1091